Table of Contents

SO-AAE-654

Amphibians

What are amphibians? They are animals that have two lives. They start life in water. Most adult amphibians live on land.

This young amphibian will grow into an adult that lives on land.

Frogs and toads lay eggs in streams, rivers, and even puddles. The eggs hatch into tadpoles. Tadpoles are born with long tails and gills. Gills help tadpoles breathe water just as fish do.

Do you see this tadpole's gills?

Soon the tadpoles grow legs. Their tails get smaller until they are gone. Lungs develop inside their bodies. Now the tadpoles can breathe air. The young frog or toad begins life on land.

Salamanders and newts are amphibians too. They are different from frogs and toads. These amphibians keep their tails.

This creature is a newt.

All amphibians have smooth, moist skin. Damp skin gives them extra air to breathe.

Endangered Amphibians

More than seven thousand kinds of amphibians hop, crawl, or swim on Earth. But many are disappearing.

This spring salamander is one of many amazing amphibians. But some amphibians are in danger.

This Hewitt's ghost frog
is endangered.

That means it's at risk
of dying out.

Hewitt's ghost frogs have sideways pupils.

The Hewitt's ghost frog lives in South Africa. You can find it near fast-flowing mountain streams. It grips wet rocks with its flat toes.

The endangered arroyo toad
lives in California. It digs a
burrow during the day.
At night, it comes out to
feed on ants
and flies.

12

The female arroyo toad lays strings of eggs. Sometimes the egg strings can reach 24 feet (7.3 meters).

Toad eggs are very tiny. These are American toad eggs.

This endangered Chinese giant salamander is the biggest salamander in the world. It lives in China and can grow 6 feet (1.8 m) long.

The Chinese giant salamander has tiny eyes. But it can feel fish moving in the water. It catches fish when it feels them moving.

This purple frog does not look much like a frog. But it is one! It doesn't live aboveground as most frogs do. It stays underground and eats termites.

Purple frogs are endangered.

15

The golden poison dart frog lives in South America. Its skin contains a strong poison. Look at the frog's greenish-gold color. Predators see its bright color and stay away.

The poison in this frog's skin can kill ten people! The poison helps this endangered creature stay alive.

Extinct Amphibians

Can you imagine a frog as big as a beach ball? The devil frog was 16 inches (41 centimeters) long and weighed 10 pounds (4.5 kilograms)!

The devil frog is extinct. That means it has died out.

The devil frog lived 60 to 70 million years ago. It may have eaten small dinosaurs.

The devil frog may have gobbled up small dinos, such as this one.

This orange-bellied newt lived in China.
It swam in the waters of Kunming Lake.

ZFMK BONN

This newt has not been seen since 1979. Underneath its greenish body is an orange belly.

People dumped waste into the waters where the Kunming Lake newt lived. The newt may have died because of dirty water.

Dirty waters like these are not safe for amphibians.

The southern day frog
lived in Australia.

This frog ate insects
during the day.

Scientists believe that southern day frogs caught a fungus. The fungus gave the frogs a disease, and the frogs died. Scientists are trying to find a cure for this disease.

Scientists study diseases to help both animals and humans.

lost their homes when people cut down too many trees.

Two Ainsworth's salamanders were discovered in Mississippi in 1964. The salamanders had no lungs. They breathed air through their skin. No other Ainsworth's salamanders have been found.

This golden toad once lived in Costa Rica. Thousands of golden toads would meet at puddles. They would mate and lay eggs. Suddenly the toads were gone. The last golden toad was seen in 1988.

Toads are usually brown or gray. Male golden toads were bright orange.

Helping Endangered Amphibians

We need amphibians. They eat insects that destroy our crops or make us sick.

Many people are trying to help amphibians. Some people keep toads safe by carrying them across roads. Others work to pass laws so stores can't sell endangered amphibians as pets. Still others clean up streams.

These people are cleaning up an area where amphibians live.

You can help amphibians too!

Learning more about amphibians is one way you can help them.

What You Can Do

There are many things you can do to help amphibians that are in danger.

- Put rocks near bushes for toads to hide under.

- Pick up trash near a lake or a pond. Clean water makes good homes for amphibians.

- Don't waste water. Amphibians need clean, fresh water.

- Take nature walks with an adult to look for amphibians.

A Remarkable Recovery

Not all endangered amphibians have to become extinct. The limosa harlequin frog has a very good chance of surviving. These tiny frogs are being raised in captivity. So far, nine frogs are hopping around in a tank. Hundreds of tadpoles swim in another tank. One day, these frogs will be set free to live in the wild.

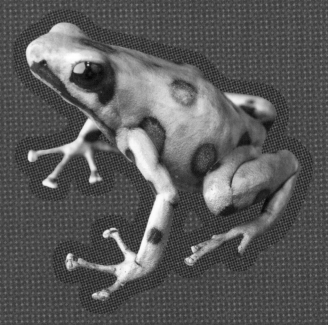

Glossary

amphibian: an animal that is born and lives in water while it is young. Most adult amphibians live on land.

captivity: a state of living in an enclosed area such as a zoo

endangered: at risk of dying out

extinct: died out

gills: body parts of fish and tadpoles that take in oxygen from water

lungs: a body part some animals use to breathe oxygen from air

mate: to produce young

predator: an animal that hunts other animals for food

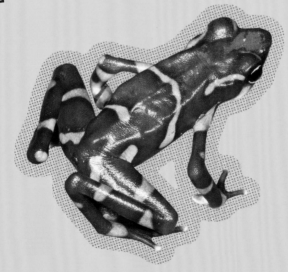

Further Reading

Berger, Melvin, and Gilda Berger. *Amphibians.* New York: Scholastic, 2011.

Enchanted Learning: Amphibian Printouts
http://www.enchantedlearning.com/coloring/amphibians.shtml

Frogland!
http://allaboutfrogs.org/froglnd.shtml

Guiberson, Brenda Z. *Frog Song.* New York: Henry Holt, 2012.

Markle, Sandra. *The Case of the Vanishing Golden Frogs: A Scientific Mystery.* Minneapolis: Millbrook Press, 2012.

Turner, Pamela S. *The Frog Scientist.* Boston: Houghton Mifflin, 2009.

Index

Photo Acknowledgments

The images in this book are used with the permission of: © Amwu/Dreamstime.com, p. 2;
© FLPA/SuperStock, p. 4; © Dirk Ercken/Dreamstime.com, p. 5; © iStockphoto.com/Valeriy
Kirsanov, p. 6; © iStockphoto.com/David Coder, p. 7; © GeoStock/Photodisc/Getty Images,
p. 8; © Michael Redmer/Visuals Unlimited/Getty Images, p. 9; © Werner Conradie, pp. 10, 11;
© Jason Mintzer/Shutterstock.com, p. 12; © Gerry Bishop/Visuals Unlimited, Inc., p. 13;
© Joel Sartore/National Geographic Stock, p. 14; © dinesh, p. 15; © iStockphoto.com/
OGphoto, p. 16; Dan Klores/Splash News/Newscom, p. 17; © Sergey Krasovskiy/Stocktrek
Images/Getty Images, p. 18; © Paul Bachhausen, www.salamanderseiten.de, p. 19; © AFP
Creative/Getty Images, p. 20; © Auscape/ardea.com , p. 21; © iStockphoto.com/Slobodan
Vasic, p. 22; © Vanessa Van Ryzin, Mindful Motion Photography/Flickr Open/Getty Images,
p. 23; © Minden Pictures/SuperStock, p. 24; © F Rauschenbach/F1online/Getty Images, p.
25; © Ambient Images Inc./SuperStock, p. 26; © Todd Strand/Independent Picture Service,
p. 27; © Zizza Gordon/Alamy, p. 29; © Dirk Ercken/Shutterstock.com, p. 30; © Tom
Brakefield/Photodisc/Getty Images, p. 31.

Front Cover: © Michael Redmer/Visuals Unlimited/Getty Images (top); © Mgkuijpers/
Dreamstime.com (bottom).

Main body text set in Johann Light 30/36.